Prais

MW01257820

"I got excited about this book because the ideas and examples were spot on. I finished reading the book because I genuinely wanted to learn more. This is how you turn around a company."

— **Brian K Heywood**, CEO/Founding Partner, Taiyo Pacific Partners LP

"Michael encourages leaders to focus on underlying, overlooked factors that can break a business, such as a company's workplace relationships and culture. By telling the story of his own successful turnaround, he shows how leaders can restore struggling organizations by investing in people and communities. This is a must-read for every business leader."

— **Verne Harnish**, Founder Entrepreneurs' Organization (EO) and author of *Scaling Up (Rockefeller Habits 2.0)*

"This book is a compelling narrative on the importance of community, communication, and trust to leadership. Michael's innovative spirit has benefited the entire Kentucky business community."

— **Ashli Watts**, President & CEO of the Kentucky Chamber of Commerce

"This book is about how strong leaders make heroes out of the people they lead. I saw firsthand how Michael rebuilt the foundations and the culture of his company. . . . Michael's patience and belief in [his team] caused the good people on the leadership team to believe in what they could do together. The process works."

— **Haydn Shaw**, veteran business consultant and author of *Sticking Points*

"This book is engaging, interesting, and spot on. The points Michael makes about culture, trust, relationships, goals, vision, and making it all have meaning are fantastic."

— **Stephanie Wachman**, Fortune 500 executive coach (Symetree Strategies) and author of *Own Your Time* and *Sell Without Being Salesy: The Power of Relational Networking*

"Building a successful business in today's world is no easy matter. Michael Rodenberg is your classic Level 5 leader who, in Bridge the Gap, has provided a fantastic resource to help you better lead and grow your business. This is a powerful resource to help you shorten your path to success."

— **Rob Grabill**, President at Chief & Senior Executive Network

"Michael's leadership has proven to be transformational, positively impacting, not only for the business but for the people and the community. His humility, servitude, and gratitude in his word and actions provide inspiration and demonstrate the heart of a true leader."

— **Susan Elkington**, President, Toyota Motor Manufacturing Kentucky, Inc.

BRIDGE THE GAP

BRIDGE THE GAP

How Leaders Can Revitalize Broken Organizations

By Michael Rodenberg

ENDEAVOR
LITERARY PRESS

Bridge the Gap: How Leaders Can Revitalize Broken Organizations

Copyright © 2020 by Michael Rodenberg

Published by Endeavor Literary Press
P.O. Box 49272
Colorado Springs, Colorado 80949
www.endeavorliterary.com

ISBN Print Version: 978-1-7358633-0-6
ISBN Ebook: 978-1-7358633-1-3

Cover design: James Clarke
Author photo: Jessica Mills

Mom and Dad,
thanks for providing a solid
foundation to build upon.

CONTENTS

Foreword		11
Acknowledgements		15
Introduction		17
Part 1: Survey the Damage		21
	1. The First Ninety Days	23
	2. Face the Brutal Truth	33
	3. Know Your Company Culture	43
	4. Engage Your Team	53
Part 2: Repair the Foundation		59
	5. Establish the Vision	61
	6. Define What Is Mission Critical	67
	7. Grow from Within	75
Part 3: Prepare for the Future		81
	8. Go and See	83
	9. Identifying Future Personnel Needs	89
	10. Establish Partnerships	95
Part 4: Open the Bridge		99
	11. Expect Greatness from People	101
	12. Give People Tools to Succeed	105
	13. Let the Horses Run	111
Epilogue		117
About the Author		121

FOREWORD

Are you in a make-or-break season of your career? Perhaps you have been given a shot to lead from the top and win big, but you realize that your business or organization is floundering. Can you bring it back to life? Or perhaps you lead a strong company and you want to keep it that way. If these are your situations, then you've picked up the perfect read.

My purpose in life is to help leaders navigate change and thrive. I've worked with hundreds of high-impact leaders. In my years of experience, I've never met anyone more able to roll with the punches and execute a growth plan—while living out of the core of who he is—like Michael Rodenberg.

Michael took on a challenging corporate turnaround assignment nearly a decade ago. He started that season equipped with rock-solid values, good instincts, and the will to win. In the growth years that followed, Michael gained wisdom that comes only through lived experience. As he revitalized a struggling company, leaders from many sectors (business, government, education, etc.) directly experienced the impact of his success. He organically grew into a sought-after public speaker and mentor. After delivering numerous talks and serving as advisor to many other leaders and boards, it was only natural for him to write this book.

What can you expect to find in *Bridge the Gap*? First, this manuscript is a practical playbook for any leader who has been called to turn around and scale-up an organization. Michael's four-principle process is easy to follow, actionable, and effective. After reading this book, you will know where to start and what to do next. You will have a roadmap to navigate the complexity that comes with leading change.

Second, you can expect to encounter a challenge. So, if you don't want to get your hands dirty as a leader, then don't read this book. Michael will challenge you to "do the things that only a leader can do." To be a "bridge the gap" leader is to be a gritty, go-and-see-for-yourself kind of leader. Too often leaders who rise to the top believe they have been exempted from the "real work." This book is an inspiring reminder to stay deeply connected to your organization so that you can earn the precious trust of your team and gain a clear understanding of your company's actual needs.

Third, by reading this book you will be reminded to focus on your purpose. Michael is a successful CEO and has the resume to prove it. The organization he leads has performed year in and year out. But leadership is about much more than that. *Bridge the Gap* asks a compelling question: "What does it profit a person to gain the whole world and lose the soul?" Throughout the book, you'll see the high purpose of leadership: honoring people and building relationships. You'll be reminded that the local community in which you are headquartered is a key stakeholder in your success; thus, if the community doesn't win, you don't win. You'll be reminded that it takes a team to accomplish anything meaningful. You'll be reminded that it's never "just business"—it's about loving people and serving your fellow humans.

Fourth, you'll enjoy reading a compelling personal story. Michael shares his heart in these pages. His transparency in storytelling is one of his best qualities. You will sense that as you read about his personal journey. You'll learn how his grandfather and other close family members and friends inspired him. You'll learn about his personal struggles and successes. In these pages, you'll meet the real guy behind the CEO title.

Finally, you'll learn that being a "bridge the gap" leader is about bringing together all kinds of people to achieve uncommon success. Michael is truly a visionary when it comes to integrating different cultures, generations, and business sectors. He's lived and worked around the world, but still prefers the small-town life. He can speak numerous languages. (It still freaks me out when he takes a call from Japan and speaks perfect Japanese.) Perhaps his global exposure enables him to see all sectors of society working together. One thing is certain: Michael models for us what it means to be a "bridge the gap" leader, which is the type of leader our world will increasingly need.

I've spent a lot of time with Michael. I know his heart and I've seen his passion to help others succeed. Take his words to heart and implement the principles put forth in this book. By doing so, you'll succeed in business, you'll discover more about who you are, and you'll bridge the gap for your team and community.

Tony Woodall
Founder and CEO of Rootstock

ACKNOWLEDGEMENTS

Without the support and encouragement of several incredible people, this book would not have been possible.

My amazing wife, Gloria, has stood by me for the past thirty years. I look forward to the next thirty.

Taro Murakami and Masaharu "Mark" Okuno, provided me with the opportunity to lead this company.

Glen Roberts, current President of MMUS, stayed when he could have gone anywhere when I walked through the door.

My executive coach and founder of Rootstock, Tony Woodall, helped me realize that I had something to share.

The entire leadership team and all the team members of MMUS have demonstrated their ability to deliver greatness. They are the inspiration behind this book.

Finally, three individuals bridged the gap for me so that I could get this book off the ground. Chuck Smith, Executive Director of Chief Executive Network, introduced me to author, speaker, and executive coach Stephanie Wachman.

Stephanie challenged me and showed me how to write what was in my head, and then she introduced me to my editor and publisher Glenn McMahan, who turned my words into a book.

INTRODUCTION

Picture an old stone bridge covered in moss and ivy that spans across a creek that winds through a forest. In the middle, supporting the arch, is the keystone. It is the most important stone. Without it, the bridge would collapse into the creek. As organizational leaders, we should serve like keystones in a bridge.

Some bridges are dilapidated. Storms, floods, and neglect have made them insecure. They could fail and fall. Restoring them so that they can be safely used requires intervention; that is, leadership.

The same is true for an increasing number of organizations and businesses. Economic crises, poor management, demoralized employees, and changing markets leave them vulnerable. Restoring them will also take leadership—keystone leaders. Without the right type of leader doing what only a leader can do, these businesses could fall apart. And that would leave a tragic gap. Clients, customers, employees, and the community as a whole would lose a valuable asset. The needs that the organization was designed to fulfill would be underserved.

The stakes are high. With the right type of leadership, neglected and struggling organizations can be restored. This book will show you how to do exactly that.

I have had the opportunity to be the "keystone" of several struggling organizations during my career. More often than not, I have been asked to help others "bridge the gap" between an existing situation and a vision for a more successful future—to help people achieve their goals.

Early in my career, while working in Japan, I learned about and gained respect for one of my company's Japanese competitors. As I followed that manufacturing firm over the years, I found out that the company was having difficulties with its North American operations. In 2011, I started working for that multinational company.

That opportunity opened up when I asked the CEO from Japan to consider me for the role of turning the North American division around. It took a little time for him to consider my unsolicited offer, but he eventually agreed. I was excited and surprised because I had never undertaken such a challenge before. I had worked in business, including in Japan, but I had never led a manufacturing company. I believed that my experience had prepared me for the job, and the parent company had yet to figure out a way to turn things around, so neither of us had anything to lose.

When I walked into the company, I had no idea what I would experience.

Or how much I would learn.

Turning around a company that had been stalled for many years taught me the four leadership principles presented in this book. They helped me bridge the gap between cultures, customers, communities, educators, and business leaders. These principles, if applied properly, can help a leader bridge gaps, moving from existing struggles to renewal and growth. The four principles are:

- Survey the Damage

- Repair the Foundation

- Prepare for the Future

- Open the Bridge

The leader is like an architect, or perhaps a structural engineer. He or she surveys the organization's problems and then repairs the foundation, serves as the keystone who holds it all up, and establishes the daily operating system (building the bridge).

My point with this analogy is that all four principles can *only be implemented by the leader,* the keystone. When we start to apply these principles, we learn that there are certain things only leaders can do. And if we don't make the most of those opportunities, our organizations will struggle to bridge the gap from where we are to where we need to go.

These four principles helped me turn around a company, build relationships between our company and the community, and change lives. My hope is that what I have learned can benefit you as much as it has benefitted me.

PART 1

SURVEY THE DAMAGE

Whenever we walk into a new situation, embark on a major transformation, or begin a new journey, we have an opportunity to step back and survey the landscape with fresh eyes. Without preconceived notions, we are free to assess the situation in a manner that will allow us to see firsthand what is taking place. Thus, the vital first step toward bridging the gap is to survey the damage.

Leaders often do not take the time to conduct an objective analysis. We feel that we must jump right into the situation and begin to work on the problems. Unfortunately, we never see the scope of the problems or the opportunities. We end up no better off than the previous leader.

Only the leader can decide to implement an objective analysis. That job cannot be delegated. And only the leader can communicate the reasons for the analysis to everyone in the organization. With proper communication, people will see what is taking place and why it is important. The elements of an objective analysis are shown below. We will look closely at each in the next four chapters.

- *The first ninety days:* This is the time that must be dedicated to surveying the organization and the key stakeholders.

- *Face the brutal truth:* Leaders must delve into the details and not be afraid of what they might find.

- *Know the organizational and team culture:* With an open mind and willingness to listen, leaders can deeply understand the culture of the organization during the first ninety days.

- *Engage your team:* Once the leader has completed steps 1 to 3, he or she should engage the team to begin implementing change.

1

THE FIRST NINETY DAYS

In 2002, I was about to complete a four-year assignment in Japan working as an expat for an American company. During those four years, I had the opportunity to meet some amazing people. I would not have had exposure to them if I had been working in the US.

One of those individuals happened to be my neighbor. He was the CEO of a Japanese automotive company who had been assigned to lead a turnaround for their alliance partner. He was a dynamic individual known for his ability to transform organizations. At that time, he was in the middle of one of the biggest corporate overhauls in the history of the automotive industry.

Knowing that I was at the end of my assignment in Japan, and that this would be a once-in-a-lifetime opportunity, I mustered the courage to ask him for career advice. He kindly said yes and invited me to his home. It was an honor to sit with him in his living room.

I had one question: What had been the secret of his success? I listened intently and took copious notes on a yellow legal pad. I could not believe that he was willing to share what he had done during each of his previous business turnarounds. His advice was simple, but profound. That night, I stuck the notes in my journal with the plan to eventually use them.

Ten years later, on the night before I started a new opportunity to lead a Japanese manufacturing company, I opened my journal and wrote down some of my thoughts. The folded yellow paper fell out. There were the notes from my meeting with the CEO from Japan. I read his advice for the first time in a decade. Those notes set in motion events that would impact my life and the lives of other people forever.

In short, they stated that I had ninety days to step back, look at the business, and conduct an objective analysis.

On the first day of my new position, the CEO and managing director of the Japanese parent company introduced me to the local team members. Following the introduction, I shared a few words, none of which I remember. Then they whisked me off to Japan for some basic training and orientation.

My initial role was to advise the Japanese CEO, who was

running the North American division, until he completed his assignment eight months later. I knew that, upon my return from Japan, I would have limited time to get things going, so I divided my plan into two phases. The first forty-five days would be devoted to surveying internal stakeholders, such as the US and Japanese management, and the local team members. The second forty-five days would focus on the external stakeholders who consisted of customers, suppliers, and the community.

Surveying Internal Stakeholders

As soon as I landed in the US, I met with the management team. Many had never met me. In our first formal meeting, I expressed my desire to learn as much as possible about the company and to determine how I might help them make progress. You could hear a pin drop. No one said a word. It was if I was speaking a different language, or as if I were from another planet.

Little did I know that some team members had been contemplating resignation. They had spent the previous ten years struggling to build product and surviving the day-to-day operations. They probably would have resigned, but the economy was emerging from the 2008 financial crisis and our company was located in a small town with few job opportunities. Prior to 2000, people in the region had endured massive layoffs when a major clothing manufacturer closed the doors on a plant that had employed more than three thousand people and that had been a community pillar. Put it this way: When it came to outsiders and big companies, the locals were not eager to trust anyone.

I realized that it was going to be challenging to build a relationship with the management team. Weak relations would complicate my ability to gather facts. In addition to them, I also had to get to know the Japanese staff who had been assigned to work in the US facility and who were acting as expat co-managers alongside many of the local staff.

I started the process by meeting one-on-one with top management, the Japanese staff, and then the leadership team. Eventually, I interviewed the team members who worked on the production floor. My goal was to understand firsthand what was going on from *everyone's* perspective.

Once I set up personal (rather than group) conversations, I realized that people were willing to share their thoughts and feelings. For many it was the first time any leader had taken the time to get to know them. Not only did we talk about work, we talked about what they liked to do, their families, and their aspirations. That experience was probably one of the most rewarding things I have ever done in my career. It is amazing what people will share if leaders are willing to listen.

At the time, I did not have a formal process to gather information. There were no surveys, forms to fill out, or specific directions. I was not trained in organizational behavior or psychology, so I was left alone to figure it out. I just asked questions and listened. I relied on my notes, despite my messy handwriting, to assess the main concerns.

While talking with the management team, I tried to understand what had gone right, what had gone wrong, what challenges still existed, and what they thought needed to change. I saw that they were extremely dedicated and hardworking individuals who wanted to do the right thing. Unfortunately, they were struggling in their work and concerned about the future. They wondered what the new guy (me) would do to fuel those anxieties. But my effort to sincerely listen to them eased some of their concerns. After meeting with each of them, I knew I had a strong group of people to work with.

The administration and manufacturing team shared similar concerns, but they demonstrated the same great qualities. I was surprised to hear how much they knew about the business. As is often the case, the people who do the day-to-day operations knew best how to make it run successfully. However, because of distrust toward management, they often held back their ideas for improvements. They knew that turnover was high due to low wages and lack of training. They knew that people cut corners. In many cases, they would tell management what they wanted to hear just to get by.

Leaders often miss opportunities to learn from the experiences and perspectives of their teams because, understandably, they are so focused on directing their organizations. But leaders need to take time to listen to people. They will tell us what is going on, especially if they feel like we are sincere and want to hear what they have to say.

Surveying External Stakeholders

After I had interviewed people within the company, I next went on the road to meet our external stakeholders. The first step was to meet with our key customers. We were fortunate because our parent company enjoyed a long-standing global relationship with them. Although, we had only been doing business in North America for ten years, the parent company had fifty plus years of history with them.

My initial visits were not pleasant. They said, "You have poor quality and you can't ship on time." That is when I knew I had problems. Had it not been for the fact that the products we manufactured were part of a global platform, our customers would have dumped us and moved on to better suppliers.

Next, I spoke with the suppliers. Many of our components came from our parent company in Japan, so we did not have many dedicated people working with local suppliers. The ones we did have were not in good financial shape. In fact, one of them went bankrupt while I was surveying the suppliers. Without a strong supply base, our business was constantly at risk.

Finally, I went into the community and tried to see how school administrators, city officials, and other people of influence viewed us. Why would I do that? Business leaders often don't realize the importance of community relations. If a company has a problem with utilities, taxes, schooling, or other public services, community leaders can be an immense help. They understand how to get things done. Moreover, they can help create a talent pipeline for hiring.

Unfortunately, I discovered that neither the Japanese nor the previous leadership team had made local relationships a priority. We had been so busy trying to keep the company alive that developing community ties was not an option. I saw that we would need to start from scratch.

The Importance of Listening

The importance of listening and honest communication can't be overstated. Halfway through the first ninety days,

I returned to Japan to provide an interim report to the parent company's senior leadership team. As I shared the report with them, I saw again how valuable open and honest communication can be in every culture. It is vital. Transparent communication helps everyone avoid basing decisions on hearsay rather than data.

Prior to delivering my report to the parent company's senior vice president, some Japanese staff members urged me to be cautious about what I would say. Knowing the vice president to be tough and firm, the staff worried that a negative report would not work out well for me. But I knew I would be the *gaijin* (foreigner), so I didn't have much to lose. I simply reported the truth as I saw it. In response, the vice president nodded as if to say, *Thank goodness someone is finally telling me what I have known all along.* I discovered that he was an experienced man who was willing to listen to the facts and not just what others thought he wanted to hear.

Unfortunately, people tend to say what they think others will *want* to hear instead of what they *should* hear. The outcome of that can be devastating. One polite falsehood leads to more falsehoods until the leaders are basing decisions on wrong information.

I encourage all leaders to take time to sincerely listen. Encourage the team to be honest. They will tell us what is going on, especially if they feel like we are sincere and want to hear what they have to say.

In summary, the first ninety days proved to be priceless. I had no idea that the advice I had received ten years earlier from my CEO friend in Japan would play such an important role. It helped me start down the path of bridging the gap.

2

FACE THE BRUTAL TRUTH

Why is it so difficult to face the truth?

When I was a child, I had to face my parents and tell them when I had done something wrong. I would pace back and forth, worry about what to say, and fear how they might react. When I finally mustered the courage to tell them what was bothering me, I was always surprised. In most cases, they would say something like, "Thanks for telling us. What are you going to do about it?"

Similar situations occur in business. Leaders and employees often worry about admitting problems. It is easier to ignore them, to brush them under the rug, rather than investigate the issues and deal with them regardless of how bad it might be. In fact, it is harder to face difficult realities in business than in personal life. Why? Problems in a business context have major financial implications—

corporately and personally—and they raise questions of status, reputation, and workplace relationships. Everyone is naturally fearful of revealing problems. But if we avoid the truth, chaos can ensue.

Chaos

After completing the objective analysis, I was able to better understand how the business was operating. Honestly, it was a mess. As I surveyed the damage, images of a seaside city recently clobbered by a category five hurricane went through my head.

As I met with the team members, a central and common theme emerged: The workers did not feel empowered to do their jobs. They were doing what they were told and not much more. If they had good ideas, they assumed (sometimes for good reason) that the Japanese management would not listen.

Moreover, there was infighting between team members and local management. A potential root of that problem was that the business was operating on the basis of hearsay instead of data. Therefore, people had conflicting perceptions about problems and solutions that were not based on solid information.

Conflict escalated and rattled good workplace

friendships. There were complaints and badmouthing and gossip. Favoritism ran rampant. There was even a terrible drug issue within the company that no one wanted to discuss, including people in key roles.

On top of all that, we also faced conflicts and distrust stemming from cross-cultural misunderstandings with the Japanese management. I was surprised to hear how frustrated the Japanese were with the Americans. They said things such as, "This plant will never succeed. They do not understand how we do it in Japan, and they are not as committed as we are to the company." The problem was cultural. The Japanese staff would work late every night, which was the norm in Japan. The American staff would leave when the day ended to be with their families. This misunderstanding eroded trust between the Japanese staff and the local staff, creating a downward cycle.

The American management team felt that the Japanese had not empowered them to do their jobs. Based on that perception, the American management team concluded that they should do the bare minimum. That was a rational conclusion, especially if they had no authority to make decisions. However, they wanted to make a difference; they just found it difficult to implement change.

Clearly this reflected a communication and cultural gap between local and Japanese management. We had to face the problem. We needed to openly communicate with one another. But the lack of mutual trust prevented us from having open and honest discussions, which was what the company so desperately needed. When I participated in the morning meetings, most discussions were about who to blame, not about how to fix a problem.

Then I dove deeply into the company data. The story became bleaker. Since the company was launched in 2000, it had had only one year of profitability. More people had been reworking or inspecting product than actually making it. There were boxes and boxes of defective products going out the door every day and into the trash. Sometimes team members would have to search dumpsters to find good product so that they could ship it to customers on time.

Obviously, this was unsustainable. The company had been able to survive for one reason: the parent company had the capital to keep it going. They had the resources, and they were also patient and persevering. They were ready to play the long game. Many other companies would have given up and moved on to something else.

I could more clearly see why our outside stakeholders were struggling to do business with us. Due to our internal chaos, suppliers could not find clear direction. Our problems flowed downhill, making it difficult for them. Because we were not leading, they could not know how to best perform to meet our requirements, and we were not able to support them.

Our company also served as a supplier. We were fortunate to have business with leading Japanese auto manufacturers. But due to our internal issues, our reputation wasn't great. In fact, workers from the companies we supplied sometimes came into our facility to provide support—so that they could get the parts they needed. For them, that was better than the prospect of problems in the supply chain.

That is not the way to establish relationships built on trust and reliability. In the auto industry, it is not easy to make big changes in the supply chain. If one company has a problem with a supplier, it could impact hundreds of other suppliers, costing everyone a fortune. That's why no one ever wants to shut down an automotive plant.

Many of our problems, described above, could be traced back to our equipment and facility layout. The company had struggled financially, so no one had taken the time or had spent the money to properly take care of the equipment. Many machines had not been properly maintained. The maintenance team had spent a lot of time chasing the same problems over and over, which had been frustrating for them. In many cases, they had known what needed to be done, but because no one had been willing to listen to their ideas, no real improvements had been made.

One major issue was our painting system. The local maintenance manager and his team knew there had been a problem with the equipment ever since the system had been installed, but (again) no one had been willing to listen to their solutions.

So, the layout of the factory was a mess. By contrast, Japanese production systems usually operated with a proper product flow that allowed employees to build product with minimal inventory. These systems also enabled leaders to address problems as needed. We, however, had the opposite outcome: The product flow resembled a spaghetti map. Whenever the company needed to expand, previous management seemed to add a new area without proper long-term planning. This created extra work and frustrated our team members.

One more huge problem emerged. With the exception of our initial groundbreaking and product launch, we had not proactively engaged with the community. As a result, the community had not understood the company's rich heritage and long history. Our name was Murakami Manufacturing USA, Inc., but on the building and on our uniforms, people only saw the letters MMUS. So, many people in the community thought there were two companies. This was a huge disappointment for me because the parent company had over a hundred years of history. Everyone in the surrounding area thought we were just another Japanese component supplier that had come to America to build parts for automakers.

Adding fuel to the community's distrust of the firm was the difficult downsizing prior to my arrival. An economic downturn had required the company to cut staff. That was hard on everyone. But, to make matters worse, the company had approached the layoffs in a somewhat random way. People who had been with the organization for years had been let go, and those with little or no experience had been retained. This diminished the reputation of the company and led top people to leave. Morale dropped so far that team members would refuse to wear anything with the company logo outside of the plant. They were embarrassed to be part of the company.

Community relations also suffered because Japanese management did not understand how to interact with local managers and staff. Many Japanese leaders had little or no experience as leaders (CEO, etc.) of a manufacturing plant. Thus, they struggled to build relationships with the staff and the broader community. Even the Americans in management roles were not given the opportunity to foster these ties, meaning that everyone lacked a true sense of partnership.

Clearly, many of the problems were not intentional or due to incompetence. The problems were often the result of cross-cultural blind spots, misunderstandings, and lackluster efforts to build strong, partnering relationships with all the stakeholders, including staff, management, and the community.

A Glimmer of Hope

How, in the midst of all that chaos, could I see hope?

As described earlier, I had spent a lot of time listening to operators, technicians, the management team, suppliers, and members of the community. Some team members I talked with had been with the company since it started. They had endured difficult situations. Many of them had previously worked at the clothing factory that had been shut down in the late nineties. They had just survived the Great Recession of 2008. I could see that they were resilient people who were eager to keep trying. Now all of them were grateful to have a job and they were willing to put up with a lot just to put food on the table. They wanted to succeed. Although morale was low, I could see that they had not thrown in the towel. That was a pleasant surprise.

I knew that every facet of the business would have major problems, but I could still see a pathway for rebuilding. I knew the brutal truth, but all was not lost. If I had lacked a clear understanding of the reality—including the hopeful aspects of the company—I might have turned away and closed shop. Surveying the situation enabled me to see the challenges as well as the opportunities.

In the early days of our company's history, the local community saw us a place of hope, a place where people could work and sustain their families. The company was *part of the community*, not separate from it. Since then, some of that reputation had dwindled. To recover our profitability and to restore relations with the community, I first needed to recover the trust and morale of the staff. The first step in that direction was to gain a better understanding of the company culture.

3

KNOW YOUR COMPANY CULTURE

One of the most obvious aspects of our company was that the owners were Japanese. Not only were they Japanese, they were very traditional Japanese who had been building products for over one hundred years. The company started as a small mom and pop shop in Shizuoka Japan making decorative metal pieces. This eventually evolved into making lanterns for the train industry. Because sheet glass was involved in that process, they started to make mirrors, which eventually led them into the furniture and construction industry. That was their history for the first sixty-five years.

In the late 1950s, the fourth-generation president of the company was approached by their sheet glass supplier and asked if he would be interested in making mirrors for the automotive industry. At the time, the glass company was making windows for Toyota Motor Company. Initially, the president did not think that mirrors on the outside of vehicles would ever become much of a business and he was leery of going into business with Toyota. (At the time, he did not know how successful Toyota would become.) But because he trusted the glass supplier, he took a chance and embarked into a business that would eventually make Murakami a global supplier of exterior mirrors.

These humble beginnings were the foundation of our company. Because Murakami was a family business, it was rich with tradition and history. They were proud of their origins and how they had grown.

When I worked in Japan, in the late nineties, I learned more about Murakami and even had the privilege of meeting Taro Murakami, who would eventually become the fifth generation CEO. I had a lot of respect for what they had accomplished, but I also saw how their traditions could be both a benefit and hindrance.

Prior to joining Murakami, I had lived in Japan as a missionary, worked for a Japanese company right out of college, and worked for several American companies that had ties to Japan. One of those companies, Donnelly Corporation, which today is owned by Magna Corporation, provided me and my family a chance to work as expats in Japan.

After finishing my missionary assignment when I was twenty-one, I had a desire to stay involved with Japan. I wanted to be in a position to take all that I had learned from the Japanese culture and figure out a way to bridge the gap between the US and Japanese cultures to make something better. Little did I know that twenty years later I would get to do exactly that during the turnaround of MMUS.

As I started the turnaround, I found it important to understand the culture within the company. Since our management team comprised Americans and Japanese, there were obviously cultural differences. Allow me to focus on three.

First, think about a double-decker hamburger compared to a single piece of sushi. In American culture, bigger is better. When many Americans go out to eat, a doggie bag for excess food is part the experience. For the Japanese, eating one piece of sushi is about more than just satisfying hunger. Sushi is an experience to be enjoyed. The taste, texture, and the presentation are all part of the eating experience. Takeout bags are not an option. In fact, if you were to ask for one in Japan, you would receive a strange look.

The second cultural difference is illustrated by comparing the cowboy with the samurai. Our company was located in the heart of central Kentucky. Many of our team members had horses, farms, and family histories dating back several hundred years to the early settlers. Many of their ancestors came to the US seeking a new opportunity. They had a dream for a better future. With a lot of grit, they carved out a place on the frontier with their bare hands. They were trailblazers, forging new things. By contrast, the Japanese samurai history, which dates back to at least AD 794, evolved over hundreds of years and was rich in tradition, honor, duty, and loyalty.

Third, compare the Western idea of "try, try, and try again until you succeed" versus the Japanese concept of *kaizen,* or continuous improvement. When I was a kid, I was told to get back up if I fell down and to not be afraid of failing. That mindset, which is common in American culture, created a sense of courage and a willingness to take chances. Perhaps for this reason so many great products have been invented in the US. By contrast, the Japanese are typically more methodical. They will plan carefully before they set out to achieve a goal. Even when the plan is complete, they will search for ways to make it better.

For example, the first videotape machine was developed in 1956 in the US by Charles Ginsburg and Ray Dolby. They were working for the Ampex Corporation at the time. But in 1969, Sony, a Japanese company, improved the technology and developed the first VCR system. The US business leaders invented the core technology and the Japanese adapted and improved it.

Another way to think about the difference between the

American and Japanese business cultures is to compare Microsoft PowerPoint and Microsoft Excel. I have sat through a lot of meetings during which the Japanese reviewed (line-by-line) a detailed plan that covered every aspect of the situation. For me, those meetings were tiresome and tedious, even though that approach increased the success rates of the plans. By contrast, my approach was to display a picture on a PowerPoint slide and tell a story. In fact, in a recent board meeting, the Japanese staff were taken aback by how I was able to tell a story that made sense and motivated them with so little information.

My point is this: Our US and Japanese cultures and business styles were distinct. Both were (and are) valid and important. We needed to tell a great story and we needed to implement a plan. So, I knew that if we could integrate the two cultures and combine their strengths, our business could achieve something great.

That integration would not be easy, in part because we had an obvious language barrier. That obstacle sometimes led to miscommunication, frustration, hurt feelings, and an overall sense of dissatisfaction. No one *meant* to cause our relational problems, but the lack of a common language easily led the Americans and Japanese to create false stereotypes of each other, further eroding healthy workplace relations.

I had learned, during my first job at a Japanese

company, that translation was not the issue; the real concern was making sure that both parties understood the *context* of each conversation. People could understand the words as they were translated, but without an awareness of the cultural context behind the words, misunderstandings and conflicts could easily occur. If distrust and confusion emerged at the management level, that distrust could infect all areas of the organization.

Unfortunately, widespread distrust had occurred in our company's management team. When I arrived, the company was in a downward spiral. But I could see that most of the misunderstandings were cultural, not ethical. As I conducted the objective analysis, it became increasingly apparent that our company culture played a key role in the health of the organization. We had to address that cultural factor in order to move in the right direction.

Know Your Team

Any organizational culture, of course, is an extension of its people. Culture is not some nebulous concept; it is a direct expression of the staff, management, and leaders. So, to gain a deep understanding of the organization's culture, leaders must get to know the people.

When I first arrived at MMUS, after a brief stint with

the parent company staff in Japan, I soon had the chance to conduct my objective analysis. I interviewed over fifty members of the team. I conversed with the US and Japanese managers, the technical staff, and those who worked on the production floor.

To conduct these interviews, I learned to ask the right questions—to help people find the freedom to speak honestly. Most people eventually felt free to do that. For many, this was the first time they had ever talked with someone at the senior management level. They found it refreshing to have an executive leader listen to what they had been through: their challenges, frustrations, and desires. The most interesting part of the interview process was meeting with the Japanese staff. No one from senior management had ever talked with them about their personal lives or taken a sincere interest in them. That approach was simply not part of their culture.

I learned that 92 percent of my team lived in one of three surrounding counties. We were the largest manufacturer in those counties and therefore central to the life of the local community. Many of these people had worked at the clothing factory prior to its shutdown. Some had farms or side businesses. Many liked to hunt and fish. Faith and family were central to their lives. (Kentucky basketball was probably most important!) Everyone had a story to tell. Some talked about their jobs, others talked about their aspirations. Many had complaints. A few gossiped.

From the management team, I learned that for the previous ten years our company had been a difficult place to work. Those who had been with the company since it started talked about their initial excitement and their eagerness to be part of something new. But once production ramped up, they realized that the company culture was not what they expected. They said that the previous senior management had been more interested in impressing their Japanese counterparts than in running the business in the best way possible.

There are always two sides to every story, and I wasn't interested in attributing blame about the past. I was more interested in knowing how everyone was doing and how they perceived our history and current situation. The more I got to know the local management team, the more they seemed like a group of puppies who had been hiding under the porch because they were not sure how they were going to be treated. When I shared that view years later with my team, they confirmed those initial impressions.

The Japanese management team had a somewhat different perspective. As part of the effort to turn the company around, the parent company sent some of their most experienced people to support me. This proved to be a huge help in making the changes, but there would still be issues.

Japanese companies typically send leaders (as expats) from the parent company as a means of supporting foreign subsidiaries. Although our company was bringing in a fresh crew, some members of the old guard were still around during the transition. Those people had various disagreements with the management team. Many of these issues stemmed from miscommunication, bad first impressions, and the inability to share honest feedback—as I described earlier. Many of the Japanese staff, who had been in the US for a long time, were technical experts with minimal management experience. They knew how to achieve results in Japan, but they had struggled to do the same in the US, in part because the people and processes (the culture) were not the same.

For example, Americans do not appreciate always being told what to do and how to do it. They would rather be taught once and then allowed to do the work independently. That is not typically the Japanese way. This cultural difference became a point of contention.

As an example, one person sent from Japan to support us was an expert in process improvements. He was confident, strong-willed, and ready for the challenge. However, I learned right away that, even though I could speak Japanese, my sense of humor could easily offend him. On one of the first days we worked together, I said something in a team meeting that was a joke. Due to language barriers, he did not understand the *context* of the joke and took it the wrong way. I, of course, apologized and we worked it out. But I realized that I needed to understand more and be more cautious during the process of building the team.

Despite these challenges, we had some amazing people on our team. Everyone wanted to do the right thing. They were willing to take a chance, and they hoped we could improve past problems. For me, this was enough to move forward with the task at hand.

Taking stock of an organization's culture is an essential but overlooked aspect of leading change and restoring thriving companies. To bridge the gap, to restore a broken business or organization, leaders need to understand the culture and assess how that culture is helping or hurting the company.

4

ENGAGE YOUR TEAM

After completing the objective analysis, facing the brutal truth, and taking the time to understand the culture of the organization, it was time to take the next step: to engage the team. I wanted to extend a challenge to them.

I had been thinking about what I could do to help the team put the past behind them and to turn their thoughts toward a positive future. We humans easily get so bogged down by our past experiences that we feel like we can't move forward. We tend to think that previous negative experiences will happen again. As described earlier, our team had had some painful experiences. They were nervous. In fact, they said, "Every time we got the courage, we would get knocked back down, so why bother."

It was hard for me to believe that people would work in such bleak conditions, but our team lived in a location with few employment options. Their situation motivated me even more to do something that could restore their confidence and help them see their potential. I wanted them to see who they were as human beings, as amazing individuals with divine DNA. To see people in that light gave me hope that I could somehow help my team see it in themselves. If I could do it for my leadership team, then they could in turn inspire others. It would not be easy, but I came up with a simple plan.

Several things from my youth came to mind. First, when I was a teenager, my father gave me the book *As a Man Thinketh* by James Allen. This short book was written over a hundred years ago. The theme is, basically, that our thoughts become our actions.

After reading the book as a teenager, I decided to picture my life five years in the future. At the time, I was living a normal life as a high school student in Temple, Texas, working part-time at the local men's clothing store and playing on a successful football team. Actually, it was more like I was warming up with the team, traveling with the team, and watching my friends play while I stood on the sidelines. If you know anything about high school football in Texas, that was not a bad place to be.

So, what did this kid from a small town in Texas envision for his life? I could see myself working in a high-rise building, wearing nice clothes, driving a nice car, and traveling around the world. I had no idea how I was going to accomplish that, but James Allen had said, "You have to think it before it will ever happen."

About five years later, when I graduated from college, my first job just so happened to be like I had imagined. That job set the wheels in motion. I knew that my thoughts could become a reality. Every five years, I would write down what I wanted to accomplish during the next five years, picture it in my mind, and then move forward with my daily tasks. Amazingly, I could look back every five years and see that what I had pictured in my mind usually came to pass.

I wanted my team to have that kind of experience. I gave each one a copy of Allen's book and asked them to read it. They probably thought I was crazy. *Why does this guy want me to read this little book?* It was unusual for a company leader to give staff members a book to read. But the next thing I did was probably even more surprising to them: I told them about my grandfather and how he used to give me fifty-cent coins.

My grandfather was a self-made man who grew up in extreme poverty with limited formal education. He was a child of the Great Depression. He went to work in the Conservation Corps and eventually joined the military and fought in World War II. Upon his return, he worked in the oilfields of West Texas and then started his own cement contracting business. He moved to Dallas, ran his business, made doll furniture, and picked up pecans to sell on street corners every year before Christmas—to make sure we all had a little extra.

He had a big influence in my life when I was a kid. He taught me how to fish, shoot a gun, and to work in his shop and at his job sites. I spent many weekends sitting in his truck eating bologna and saltine crackers as we sold the doll furniture he had made in his shop.

During all this time, he would give me fifty-cent coins. He had a collection of them in his gun case. These coins meant a lot to me. They symbolized my grandfather as a man who persevered to make something of himself, even when the odds were stacked against him. He was someone who lived what James Allen talked about, even though he had never read the book.

The Fifty-Cent Piece Challenge

The book and my grandfather's story inspired me to extend the "fifty-cent piece challenge" to my team, as a means of engaging them in our next business steps. I gave each person on the local and Japanese leadership team a fifty-cent coin and a copy of the book. I challenged them to read the book and told them to keep the coin with them at all times. I also encouraged them to use the coin as a frequent reminder to consider their mindset, to ask themselves, *Am I thinking about ways to become better at my job, and about being a better spouse and parent?* I wanted them to realize that the past did not matter. The key was to focus on improving today. I wanted them to picture our business five years from today. I wholeheartedly believed that if their thoughts were focused on something good, they would end up doing it.

I extended this challenge with the hope that they would see the business in a new light, that they could imagine it as a place where they enjoyed working. I knew it would be tough, but I believed in my heart that they were capable of doing great things. Fortunately, no one thought I was crazy, and almost everyone was willing to accept that challenge.

PART 2

REPAIR THE FOUNDATION

"The wise man built his house upon a rock," said Jesus.

Without a strong foundation, a building will not stand the test of time. For an organization, that foundation does not consist of concrete or stone; it is based on something much stronger: trust. Businesses are run by people, not machines; therefore, trust must exist for businesses to flourish. Patrick Lencioni taught that the lack of trust will result in a dysfunctional team, so in order to build a strong team, trust must be the foundation.

In this section of the book, we look at three important aspects of repairing and rebuilding an organization's foundation.

- *Establish the vision:* Leaders need to determine and then convey a clear vision for the organization, one that can be understood and easily implemented by everyone.

- *Define what is mission critical:* The leadership team must identify and invest in mission critical processes and people.

- *Grow from within:* Every great organization requires excellent, committed team members. This chapter describes how leaders can invest in and develop people who already work in the company.

5

ESTABLISH THE VISION

The foundations of great organizations are, I believe, initially based on words. Take for example the *Declaration of Independence*. The writers of this document had a vision for the United States. They knew that in order for it to stand the test of time, they needed words to define and express the core ideology and direction.

As we set out to restore our struggling company, we needed to rewrite our vision, goals, and actions—to define our identity as a company and express what we stood for as individuals and as a group. These statements needed to be simple and direct, enabling us to easily talk about them in our conversations. We wanted them to become part of the fabric of our culture and, collectively, become a framework for how we operated our company.

As the new company leader, it fell mostly to me to lead

the process. I felt that I would need divine help to come up with a written foundation for the organization. My heart-felt motivation was to help others achieve their goals, to inspire them to do better, and even to help them to get through the day.

After a lot of prayer, and hours of writing and rewriting, and with the help of my team, we developed the vision, goals, and actions statements that we still live by today. These statements include three elements: why we exist, what we do, and how we do it.

Vision: Why We Exist

The vision of Murakami Manufacturing USA, Inc., is to be known by our customers as their "supplier of choice" and to be known by the community as the "employer of choice." When we wrote our vision statement, our reality was the opposite. So, the vision statement challenged us and enabled us to see a distant goal, something we could aspire to. The best part of the vision was that it was simple: "supplier of choice" and "employer of choice."

What did it mean for us to become the "supplier of choice"? It meant that our customers would prefer coming to our company above all others to supply their business needs. In the automotive industry, accomplishing that is next to impossible because customers must avert risk and not place all their eggs in one basket. But we wanted them to be disappointed if they could not select us as their supplier.

To be an "employer of choice" was also a lofty vision. We wanted people in our community to know us as the best place in the region to work. We wanted our team members to be proud of their company, and we wanted to make a positive impact in our community. This part of our vision was interrelated with the first part (being the best supplier). If we wanted to exceed the expectations of our customers, we needed to be a great place to work, a place with the best people.

Goals: What We Do

The statement of our goals gave us clarity about what we needed to do in order to fulfill our vision. Our goals were to safely deliver quality products and generate sustained profits so that we could support our customers and provide a livelihood to our team members for many years.

During the first eleven years of company history, not many goals had been achieved. Our safety record was poor, our customer quality was not acceptable, and there had only been one profitable year since the company was established. That type of situation would not provide a long-term livelihood for our team members. Our new goals statement helped us focus on what to do to turn the company around.

Actions: How We Do It

Finally, our actions statement would become central to our organization. This statement clarified how we would work together. The statement included: work safely; build quality products; protect the environment; operate to Key Performance Indicators (KPI); establish a culture where greatness is expected, remembering that *kaizen* (continuous improvement) is a way of life and that treating others with respect and care is the standard.

Several parts of this statement mean a lot to me. The first is to operate to KPIs. When I first arrived at the company, I noticed that every discussion was based on hearsay. When there were problems, people would tell me that it was someone else's fault and that I needed to fix it. That needed to end. I started asking people to bring me data that supported their complaints. At first, people were not sure how to react. The company had plenty of data, but no one knew how to use it.

My next favorite element of the statement was to expect greatness. To inspire greatness, we all had to expect it. This was a major culture shift in the company. Previously, not too much had been expected from the team, except to do what they had been told to do. Now, by expecting greatness, we had to provide them with clear expectations and then let them run. Once they understood the expectations, they were able to do great things.

Next, the idea of making *kaizen* a way of life and treating people like they wanted to be treated was significant. *Kaizen*, or continuous improvement, expressed our Japanese roots. It inspired people to get better than they were the day before. By creating a culture with *kaizen*, our accomplishments could be unlimited. Likewise, by treating others as we would want to be treated, we could greatly improve our workplace relationships and become a great place to work. If people weren't treated with respect, we would eventually lose excellent staff. In the early days of implementing these foundational statements, this element seemed like it would be the hardest to achieve.

These statements became more than wall decoration; they became the foundation of our business. Whenever we faced a difficult situation, they helped us decide which direction to go. Everything we did centered on becoming a "supplier of choice" and an "employer of choice." We did not waste our time or resources on anything else. In the next chapter, I address more specifically how we made "mission critical" decisions.

6

DEFINE WHAT IS
MISSION CRITICAL

The most vital organ in the human body is the heart. If it stops, everything else will stop. Likewise, every organization has something equivalent to the heart. If it does not operate properly, the organization will not reach its maximum potential. That "something" in a company can also be called a "mission critical" function. In order to set a new, strong foundation for a company, leaders must identify and focus on mission critical areas.

When I joined our company, it didn't take long to identify what was mission critical. We make exterior mirrors for automotive manufacturers. Drivers use our mirrors every few minutes as they travel down the road. Over the past sixty-five years, the mirror has evolved from a metal frame with a small round mirror into a complex product with over 130 highly engineered components that are injection molded, painted, and then assembled with lights, electronics, and (now) cameras.

As I reviewed our processes, it became obvious to me that we were spending a lot of time and money on inspecting and reworking our painted injected parts, including parts that had already been inspected. Instead of improving the manufacturing processes, we were spending all of our time trying to find and fix our mistakes.

Two processes were mission critical. Injection molding required that the tools, materials, and equipment be maintained to exact specifications. If no one paid attention to that process, or if the equipment and tools were not properly maintained, then we ended up with defective parts. It's just like a heart: If a person doesn't exercise, eat well, and get checkups, he or she will eventually have issues.

Sometimes our defective injected parts would flow to our paint process, which was even more complex than the injection molding process. Painting materials and equipment needed to be monitored constantly. One mistake could mean the loss of an entire batch of product. Unfortunately, we could see that our inspectors were surrounded by stacks of defective or poor-quality product.

The injection molding and paint processes were clearly mission critical, so we had a significant problem. We were generating approximately $100,000 a month in scrap material, and we had fifty people assigned to inspect and repair the poor-quality product. If we could stabilize those two areas, we could dramatically improve our business. So, as a team, we decided to dedicate most of our time and resources to improve the injection molding and painting processes.

Every organizational leadership team can choose to focus on mission critical areas. It starts with asking, "What is the heart of our business?" Once the team knows what is mission critical and what isn't, they can focus energy on that area to make improvements and change the direction of the company.

Who Is Mission Critical?

I have so far defined "mission critical" in relation to processes. However, a process requires human interaction. Even in today's world of automation and artificial intelligence, there are people behind the scenes who make it all happen.

In our case, we had identified the mission critical processes, but we still needed to determine *who* was mission critical—the skilled people who made these processes function. Our processes required people who had acquired specialized skills through extensive training.

We could not just post a help wanted sign and expect people with those skills to show up at the door. We had to search for them and train them. We often realized our vital need for skilled workers if someone with all the knowledge walked out the door and left us scrambling to figure out how to even turn on a machine.

As technology continues to rapidly change, positions that require highly skilled people have become increasingly critical to the success of our organization. In order to fulfill our vision, we decided to focus more on understanding our needs for these roles.

Cultural differences influenced this decision. Japanese business leaders traditionally don't think about mission critical roles because people usually work at the same place for their entire lives. Staff are often paid according to years of service, not levels of skill. As older people with knowledge depart, younger people are trained to fill their spots. Also, Japanese businesses have many generalists because people can move from one department to another after only a few years. So, for the Japanese in our management team, the concept of mission critical positions was foreign. The US management team had to lead the way.

First, we had to identify which roles were mission critical. In our company, those people had technical backgrounds. They were technicians who worked on the injection tools, molding and painting processes, and crucial assembly equipment. They understood the equipment required for those processes, and the characteristics of the materials. Without people like them, we could not make good parts.

In 2011 and early 2012, when the US was coming out of the Great Recession, skilled technicians were readily available. Manufacturing was starting to pick up steam, but there was not a huge demand in the market for technically trained staff. This economic context enabled us to identify and hire some good people, but we also needed to protect those positions. At the time, only thirteen of our 350 team members were technicians. Their knowledge and experience allowed us to make good products, and we didn't want to lose them even as we hired new people.

We also needed a system to make sure we had a long-term ability to hire qualified workers. How could we be sure that the applicants were in fact qualified? Anyone could walk in the door with a resume and claim to have technical skills or even fool us by using the right words. While keeping our eyes focused on our KPIs, we came up with a way to evaluate the true skills of our applicants.

We began working with a local technical college to develop a method to test the capabilities of our technical staff, potential new hires, and students who were about to graduate. After some initial skepticism, everyone saw that our approach opened opportunities. We could then objectively evaluate the skills of experienced technicians, and we could understand the capacities of new younger workers. In addition, we could identify their weaknesses and help them improve their skills faster.

We also developed a way to compensate them based on their knowledge and in relation to local market trends. We did not want these people walking out the door. Because we only had thirteen techs at the time, increasing their wage scale would not have a significant impact on our cost structure. But our Japanese members found this idea difficult to consider. For them, wage increases should be based on years of service, not on job knowledge and technical ability. Ultimately, I was able to proceed with the wage increases because the Japanese parent company had given me authority to make major changes.

We took one additional step to protect these mission critical roles. In the past, the technicians were only expected to come in, do the job, not make mistakes, and then go home. Now, as part of our actions statement, we wanted a culture where greatness was expected and where continuous improvement was a way of life. The equipment and technology were changing, so we wanted to make sure we could offer them ongoing opportunities to improve their skills.

As a result of implementing these actions, our techs have become some of the most savvy and smart people in our business. They like to grow, and they know that getting better every day will lead to increased income. Many of my technicians drive bigger trucks and have much nicer boats than me! I am totally okay with that because they are mission critical workers. I want to make sure we can keep them in our company for years to come.

In 2011 we had approximately 340 team members, thirteen techs, and approximately $50 million in revenue. Eight years later we had 340 team members, including thirty techs, and approximately $100 million in revenue.

Knowing what and who is mission critical is vital to the success of any business.

7

GROW FROM WITHIN

I played basketball when I was a kid. Although I was not the most talented guy on the team, I had one thing going for me: height. My coach told me he could teach me to dribble, pass, and shoot, but he couldn't teach me to be tall. That was true, but he failed to mention that there would be much taller boys than me who had better skills. My basketball career was rather short lived.

In business, leaders can teach a person how to do a specific task and how to manage people, but leaders can't teach what only years of experience can provide. Experience provides understanding, patience, and wise thinking that all companies need. Without experienced people, restoring a struggling organization is likely to fail.

So, the second element of setting a strong company foundation is to find people with extensive experience.

Doing so can be a challenge because experience is acquired over time through many successes and failures. Moreover, individuals need to learn from and make the most of their experiences. Simply working the same job for twenty years does not necessarily make a person wise.

As I began the turnaround of MMUS, I did not have a team to bring with me, and I knew it would be difficult to find experienced leaders to join me in the middle of Kentucky. But I knew that I had a lot of untapped talent within the organization. So, I decided to set the foundation by promoting people from within the company, people who had experience and who were willing to learn.

This proved to be a key factor in becoming an "employer of choice." By promoting from within, I sent a message of hope to our existing staff. Prior to my arrival, most leadership roles had been filled by people from the outside or by Japanese staff sent from the parent company. Therefore, local staff never saw many opportunities for growth or personal development. I looked for experienced people within the company and then helped them blossom into leaders. We identified people who wanted to grow and learn, and then we provided them with opportunities to advance in their careers.

One talented young man, who was a little rough around the edges, had some difficulty keeping company rules. His appearance and attitude gave everyone the impression that he was a rebel. I told him that he could take the next three days off without pay and use the time to determine if he wanted to be part of my team. Three days later he came back a changed person. He went from causing problems to solving problems. Today he plays a vital role in the success of our business. This young man had experience that, once channeled in the right direction, enabled him to be a light to others.

A few years before I arrived, due to a downturn in the economy, the company had to downsize. Unfortunately, the company lost some experienced people. The downsizing had severely impacted individuals and the community, in part because many of them had gone through layoffs when the clothing factory closed in the late nineties.

After a few years as CEO of the company, I had the opportunity to rehire one of those people. After the downsizing, she furthered her education. As it turned out, I needed someone with her education. I was also excited to hire her because she already understood the business and was from the local community. Our company benefited from a person who would eventually play a big part on my leadership team.

Nearly every person on my leadership team today has "grown up" within the company. They have a variety of backgrounds that have allowed them to make a significant impact on the business. Regardless of where they started, they all progressed in the business and gained a lot of knowledge. That experience has helped them become excellent leaders.

Growing people from within is remarkable. Like I mentioned before, you cannot teach experience, but you can teach experienced people how to lead. To do that, we helped our people embark on a variety of learning journeys. For example, I asked the management team to read Patrick Lencioni's book titled *Five Dysfunctions of a Team*. My maintenance manager came up to me and said, "Wow! This guy wrote a book about us." It was exciting to watch people embrace a process of personal improvement beyond just doing their jobs.

I also invited an executive coach to help us. I found a young man, Jeremy Taylor, who had been raised in the region. He was establishing a leadership development business. We did our first off-site session with him, which was a new experience for our team. Jeremy helped us get outside of our comfort zones and to look at each other not as mere co-workers, but as individuals with different talents and abilities. The coaching session was a key turning point in developing the business.

Next, we took our managers through Franklin Covey's one-year program called the Speed of Trust. I evaluated a variety of programs before I chose Covey. The other programs were good, but this program was scalable and could be taken to other operations throughout the world. We brought in a great coach and author, Haydn Shaw. He was able to teach the team about the Speed of Trust, changing many of their lives forever. To this day I think it was the best thing we ever did as a company.

These stories about training leaders relate to my analogy about height. Our management team knew the ins and outs of the business, but no one had ever taken the time or invested the money in their own personal and leadership development. When those soft skills are taught to a team who already understands the business, they quickly become more effective in day-to-day tasks.

For these reasons, I strongly believe that growing leaders from within is a critical part of repairing the foundation of a struggling organization. It is crucial for senior leaders to determine how to help emerging leaders get to the next level. If they grow, the business will also grow.

Building New Leaders by Investing in the Community

I'm not suggesting that leaders should *only* invest in people who already work in the company. Leaders can and should recruit local people. Doing so is one way that an organization can invest in the future of a local community while also finding good employees.

As I started the company turnaround, I was asked to serve on the board of the Kentucky Chamber Workforce Center, a group established to "bridge the gap" between education, business, and government. Learning about some social issues in the state inspired me to do more to help. For example, workforce participation in our state was the eighth lowest in the nation and the incarceration rate was the ninth highest. Opioid overdose deaths were the fourth highest, and the disability rate was the fourth highest in the nation. These problems did not directly impact my life, so why should they bother me?

Well, they did bother me. As I studied the data more closely, I realized that many people facing severe hardships would benefit from working for our company. They needed good jobs. Rather than complain about how no one wanted to work or about how everyone was on drugs, I began looking for ways to be a part of a solution.

PART 3

PREPARE FOR THE FUTURE

When I was a kid, I never thought that I would someday be the CEO of a company, and I never thought I would be the father of five and eventually a grandfather. These wonderful opportunities did not just happen; they were the results of years of preparation.

Most of us have heard the phrase, "If you are prepared, you shall not fear." The same is true for organizational leaders. In this third section of the book, we look at how to "bridge the gap" by taking the time to prepare for the future. Doing so will give us a much greater chance of revitalizing our organizations. We'll address three more elements of how organizational leaders can bridge the gap, transforming a struggling company into a profitable and influential business.

- Like a military scout checking out the land before a battle, the principle of "go and see" can enable leaders to more clearly identify new opportunities— to better envision the future of the company and help prepare for that future.

- Thriving businesses in rapidly changing times need qualified personnel, people who are equipped to embrace new technologies and processes. Thus, leaders need to have a long-term approach for creatively recruiting those people.

- Why carry all the weight alone? To establish a strong foundation for the future, leaders should develop partnerships with schools, government agencies, and community organizations in mutually beneficial ways.

8

GO AND SEE

No human being, despite all the charlatans out there, can predict everything that might happen in the future. So, how can we prepare for a future that we can't see very clearly?

Well, thankfully, we can see ahead to some degree, if we are willing to get out of our own bubbles and learn. We can read books and articles by industry leaders and we can stay in tune with technological trends, and we can keep an eye on economic directions. But an often-overlooked way to learn more about the future is to spend time with other leaders and companies to see what they are doing. I call this the "go and see" principle.

When I started at Murakami, I learned this approach from one of my bosses and mentors. His name was Masuharu "Mark" Okuno. He had been in the automotive industry for many years at the Toyota Motor Corporation Upon his retirement from Toyota, he joined our company Mark had worked for Toyota Canada and had been responsible for launching the first Lexus vehicle built in North America, as well as other important vehicles.

I knew that Mark, due to his extensive experience, could help me see the future—ways to improve what we were currently doing. As Mark and I walked through our plant, he had me pick up a vehicle mirror and examine it. He pointed out that there were fingerprints all over the mirror. This mirror was destined for the Lexus plant! I had not paid much attention to that detail, because I figured that the vehicle would be washed many times before it got to the customer. So why worry about fingerprints?

Mark explained that a Lexus product was different. The Lexus company motto was "the pursuit of perfection." To them, every part was important. Knowing that, Mark believed that the Lexus assembly worker who took our product out of the box should have a good experience. This type of thinking had been beyond my comprehension.

Then Mark took me to Toyota Canada so that I could "go and see" the production floor and watch firsthand how the company built its vehicles. From the moment I walked through the plant doors, I knew something was different. The employee entrance resembled a luxury Lexus dealership: hardwood floors, decorative walls, and a vehicle on display. I was blown away as soon as I walked into the building. As I went out on the floor, I saw team members dressed in various Lexus uniforms. The plant was extremely clean. Everyone worked hard to build a perfect vehicle.

From that day forward, my attitude about how to present our mirrors to our customers changed. We still make mistakes, but we take a lot more care than before. Our Lexus assembly line is now different than any other line in the plant and our people work with the Lexus mindset. I will be forever grateful to Mark for helping me see one aspect of our future—improved attention to details that meet customer needs and wants.

My point is this: Had I not applied the "go and see" principle, I would have continued with a status quo mindset. I have continued to apply it when I encounter new problems and in different contexts. For example, in 2013, a local principal from our technical high school, Linda Floyd, visited my facility and invited me to "go and see" what her students were doing in the classroom. I hadn't been in a high school classroom since I last attended a parent-teacher conference, so I decided to accept her invitation.

I saw young people engaged in learning and building products out of scrap materials. They were so excited and focused that I could picture them as future team members and leaders in our company. I saw how wrong it was for anyone to think that tech schools were places for kids who weren't good enough to go to college or who didn't have a "real" future.

During my visit, I remembered that I had over $100,000 in obsolete material— harnesses, motors, lights, etc.—sitting in a warehouse. We had planned to dispose all of it soon. I realized that these kids could probably use most of it. A few days later it was delivered to the school.

A few weeks later, I went back to see whether the school was putting it to good use. What I saw amazed me. Those kids had built giant robots out of material once considered junk. The experience fortified my belief in the power of "go and see." By taking the time to look around, I discovered something amazing and met some remarkable young people.

The "go and see" principle can give leaders a broader vision for the future. I believe it is the leader's responsibility to apply it. If I had sent my HR manager to the school in my place, she might not have seen what I saw. She would have seen great kids doing great things, but she might have missed the big picture, and she would not have had the authority to implement what I could do as the business leader. By comparison, I could envision future team members, and I knew that our obsolete material could be put to good use while giving us a tax deduction. By making a sizeable donation, I believed we could build stronger community relations, which was part of our vision to be the employer of choice. As the company leader, I could see individual pieces fitting into a broader whole. Only a leader can do that.

The "go and see" principle is one of the most critical aspects of preparing for the future. As leaders seek to bridge the gap—restoring businesses to success— we need to constantly see ways to gain a clearer picture of the future. Without that, how can we know how to get to the other side?

9

IDENTIFYING FUTURE
PERSONNEL NEEDS

When I feel hungry because I didn't take the time to eat breakfast, or when I am dehydrated because I didn't drink enough water, or when I'm stressed, I often run to the snack machine for a soda and a candy bar. Obviously, that approach doesn't solve my long-term need for real nutrition; it's a short-term fix that makes matters worse.

The same type of outcome can occur when leaders try to address *real* needs with stopgap measures. We often take the dartboard approach: throwing things at the wall and hoping that one will hit the target. We should instead take some time, step back, and focus on the situation. We should do what is required to understand the organization's real, long-term needs so that we can prepare adequately for the future.

A primary long-term need for every company is personnel—finding and retaining high quality people to operate the company. But, in my experience, leaders neglect to study which positions they will need to fill in the long-term future. That happened to us about two years into our turnaround. We had done a good job of identifying the mission critical processes and people, and our investments in those areas allowed us to stabilize the business. However, we then realized that we needed to think about our future needs. We knew that we had to step away from the daily battle and take a long look into the future.

We soon began to see the potential for serious personnel shortfalls. First, we saw that we did not have a very deep bench. The team we had in place did a spectacular job of taking care of the business, but if one of them became ill or, worse, left us to pursue a better opportunity, we would immediately be unable to staff our mission critical processes. To avoid falling back into our old ways, we needed to immediately build a more equipped "bench."

Second, we saw that most of our all-star players were veterans. They had many years of service under their belts, experience that could not be transferred to new people overnight. Their expertise had been acquired through years of problem solving and trial and error. I knew they only had a limited amount of playing time before they would hang up their tools and go on to other adventures. So, I needed to figure out how to hire a second string and encourage the veterans to train them.

My long-term goal was to develop the next generation of superstars. We knew that times were changing fast and that new opportunities were on the horizon. We knew that technology was advancing and that many of our veterans did not have experience with the new processes and tools that would become available in the future. Filling this gap—to prepare for the future—would not be easy. We had to develop a new generation of mission critical technical staff.

But how?

The Power of One by One

Due to the nature of our business, we had experienced periods of high turnover and rapid growth. In either case, there were times when we needed an additional twenty people in short order. In a down labor market, that was not a big deal. We would post the job and thirty people would show up. We would train them, and the problem would be solved. I believe those days are over. When it comes to hiring and developing new people, *as a means of preparing for the future,* it is all about one person at a time. In a tight labor market, it is a lot easier to find one person twenty times than it is to find twenty all at once.

In order to find one person at a time, we needed a creative approach. Using the normal hiring agencies provided some support, but that put us up against other employers who were receiving applications from the same people who applied with us. We had to think outside the box.

We first started to hire people part-time. We sought individuals who wanted to work but who, due to their schedules, could never work full-time in manufacturing. That led us to start building relationships with local high schools, technical schools, and universities. We hoped to create a pipeline for people in our region, giving them an opportunity to work while going to school. By giving them work opportunities, we hoped they could stay in the area, establish homes, and start families; in other words, to invest in the local community.

We created unique programs, such as RQ1, which was developed to help people who did not have a high school diploma or GED. In this program, these people could work for us while they completed basic education requirements. It was not a huge success, but it created opportunities for a few people who otherwise would not have had the opportunity to work.

Then there was "Murakami Next Gen." This program emerged from the "go and see" experience I described earlier. While serving on the Kentucky Workforce Center board, I received data that showed that a high percentage of the state's high school graduates had never completed any post-high-school education. Further study revealed a lot about the private universities that became the inspiration for the program. We wanted to target high school seniors and hire them to work for a defined period of time. It was a unique program that received great feedback from educators. The program enabled us to hire students who normally would not be able to work in manufacturing and then help them with their future life plans.

When the unemployment rate was extremely low, we also recruited hourly workers. At that time and in our region, this approach was unheard of. Most hourly workers in other companies usually lost benefits and seniority if they changed jobs. They would have to start at the bottom and work their way up again, which could often take up to five years. So, hiring on an hourly basis was a huge barrier to recruiting skilled individuals.

We tried a new approach. We realized that there was no difference between hiring a person for an office job and hiring someone for an assembly job. Both jobs were important. So, we targeted people from our community who had to drive long distances to get to work. Word got out and all of the sudden our job fairs were filled with people.

These are just a sample of all the things we did to find one person at a time. We were not always successful, but we were able to find good people who have contributed to the success of our company.

Leaders must look at the big picture. But when it comes to people, leaders need to see that every individual is important. If we lose sight of that, we will miss out on opportunities, not only for company growth, but also for the improvement of communities. To prepare for the future, we must see the importance of investing in one person at a time.

10

ESTABLISH PARTNERSHIPS

How much can you accomplish on your own?

Recently I had to move some outdoor plants for my wife. I soon realized that if I tried to lift the plants alone, I would end up with a back injury. Then I remembered that my sixteen-year-old son was hanging out in the house, so I asked him for help. He agreed and the job was complete in a few minutes. The simple act of involving my son made my life easier and probably made him feel good because he was able to help me. Why don't we do this more often? Why are we so afraid to ask others for help?

When it comes to preparing a foundation for the future of an organization, I'm convinced that developing strong partnerships is crucial.

When I joined MMUS in 2011, my team and I first tried to move plants without outside help. We did everything on our own. When I suggested that we should develop better relationships with the local mayor, county judge, and economic development director, they looked at me like I was from another planet. "Why would you reach out to them?" they replied. "Those people would probably just ask us to do something for them." But I saw them as people who could help us when we had a problem in the community or with local resources.

The same applied to our relationships with local schools. We did not have any relationships with superintendents, principals, or other education leaders. But I saw the schools as a potential pipeline for our future employees.

As I mentioned earlier, Linda Floyd from the Green County Area Technical Center had asked me to "go and see." That interaction opened the door for me to develop stronger relations within the local school system. They wanted to hear my opinion about how they could better serve our business. They wanted students to hear about my experiences in business, and they wanted me to open our company doors so that students and teachers could see what we were doing. Local educators (and many others in our community) had never seen the inside of our manufacturing plant. Whatever they heard from the local rumor mill was all they knew about us.

Each of these situations provided an opportunity for our company to build partnerships that bridged the gap between business, education, and government. We invited the local city council, high school principals, teachers, and the Chamber of Commerce to visit our facility. Everyone took an interest in our business and became sources of information about what was taking place in the community. None of this took much effort, but it benefitted everyone tremendously, including us.

I also regularly made time to visit people outside of our community. I went to high schools in the surrounding counties, to suppliers, and to some major universities in larger cities. Each of these visits led to something good.

At the University of Louisville, I met Dr. Sudar Atre, who headed up a department focused on additive manufacturing, which is a fancy term for 3D printing. Dr. Atre introduced me to his students and showed me around the department. I was amazed at the students and what they were doing. This led to some collaboration. Dr. Atre and our mutual friend, Kevin Shurn, and I led a presentation for the Workforce Development Council for the US Conference of Mayors in Washington, DC. This partnership eventually enabled us to hire several of his students and help other students land jobs with our suppliers.

While visiting our suppliers, I discovered a company that was similar to ours. That company was also Japanese-owned, and it faced many of the same challenges we had faced. I invited the president, Keisuke "Keith" Hagiwara, to visit our plant and I shared our recovery plan with him. I then met with his leadership team at his facility. A few years later, he invited me back and showed me how they had turned around the company based on what they had learned from working with us.

Finally, I asked a school principal if she wanted to bring her students to our plant. She replied that she lacked funding. When I learned how much it would cost to rent a bus and hire a substitute teacher, I was shocked: about $300. That experience led to a statewide program called Bus2Business. We created this program in partnership with the Kentucky Chamber Workforce Center, where I served on the board. Just a few months after my meeting with that principal, we had thousands of students in Kentucky visiting companies for the first time.

With little expense, leaders can establish partnerships with a wide range of people in government, education, or other businesses. The benefits are mutual. New initiatives can sprout from one experience. We never know what we might learn from someone else.

When it comes to preparing for the future, it's better to carry the plants together.

PART 4

OPEN THE BRIDGE

After we have conducted our objective analysis, worked to build our foundation, and turned our energies toward preparing for the future, we can focus on the fourth phase of bridging the gap. In this section, we will address how to apply the principles described in sections 1 to 3.

Waking up every day is a blessing. Anything can happen. It's also possible that each day could be the last of this mortal existence. So, what are we choosing to do with this day? Are we living it to the fullest? Are we leaving our mark on those around us so that we can be remembered as someone who cared? We do not know what the next minute, hour, or day might bring, but if we recognize that we only get today, then we can begin to see all the ways to bridge the gaps in our lives, in the lives of others, and in our businesses.

In this final section of the book, I discuss three ways that leaders can bridge the gap to revitalize businesses and help them flourish for years to come.

- When leaders expect greatness from their teams, people experience dignity and self-worth that inspires them to reach their full potentials, thereby making better contributions to the company.

- To succeed, leaders need to make sure that their teams have the right tools for their jobs.

- Finally, leaders should "let the horses run." Team members need freedom to work according to their natural talents and personalities and cultural backgrounds. Giving people freedom builds morale and increases success.

11

EXPECT GREATNESS
FROM PEOPLE

Someone once told me, "If you expect nothing, you get nothing, but if you expect greatness you will get it." That idea has had a profound impact on my life. As we were writing our company's vision, goals, and actions, the words "expect greatness" came to mind, perhaps because as a child I had been taught that people are sons and daughters of a living God and thus have divine DNA. This truth helps me to see people not as they are today, but as they can become. Unfortunately, many people can't see that truth about themselves.

My first experiences at the company were challenging because a culture of "expect greatness" did not yet exist. In fact, we had a culture of "keep your head low and do whatever it takes to survive." That type of culture can breed mistrust and disloyalty. People can tend to look out for themselves and, in some cases, to lead by fear and control Individuals in this type of environment can feel forced to suppress who they really are. They take on characteristics that go against their true natures.

During the initial phases of our company revitalization, I had the opportunity to get to know many amazing people who did not realize how great they were. They were talented people, but for some reason, others had not seen their potential. It would be difficult to share all my stories because each one is unique. So, I will just share one.

We had a supervisor in one of our manufacturing departments who was tough and could get things done. She worked hard and took pride in her work. However, she tended to pick favorites. Sometimes she pushed the limits on how she treated others. I eventually had to ask her to take a few days off and to think about what she wanted to do.

When she returned, she had a sincere desire to do better. Over time, I watched her change. Her sharp edges softened, and she became more compassionate with everyone. She took corrective criticism in a manner that allowed her to grow. And she started to lead with greater purpose. Her skills increased and she took on new challenges. Instead of leading by hearsay, she began using data. She gained the trust of her entire department and of the management team. Eventually, she accepted a key role at another company. When she left, I was proud of what she had accomplished, and I looked forward to seeing the next chapter in her life.

When I first met her, I saw that she had something unique. By expecting something great from her, she eventually showed her true colors and delivered greatness. If I had listened to the people who said she would never change, I would have missed an amazing experience.

This individual, as well as many others, had what I call *height:* the qualities that can't be taught. As I mentioned earlier, people can be taught to read, to lead, and to do specific tasks, but they cannot be taught certain character traits. The person described above had character, but she didn't have anyone who expected greatness from her.

All people have some form of "height." However, if someone doesn't help them realize all they can be, they can go through life without reaching their full potential. I enjoy expecting greatness from people because it helps them achieve great things. Watching people live up to their potential is, for me, an amazing aspect of this life.

That is why I enjoy talking to groups of young people. When I walk into a room of students, I see so much potential. The problem is that *they* don't see it. When I ask them, "What are you thinking about?" many respond by saying "nothing." So, I challenge them. "If you are thinking about nothing, you will end up doing nothing, but if you are thinking about doing something great, you will most likely do it." This is not about perfection, I add; it's about doing better each day.

Leaders must expect greatness from our team members, otherwise we will miss opportunities to help our people realize their full potential. And, as a result, our organizations might never reach their maximum capacities.

12

GIVE PEOPLE TOOLS
TO SUCCEED

I am one of the cheapest people in the world. Just ask my wife. It pains me to spend money on anything. Maybe my grandparents, who grew up during the Depression, transferred a penny-pinching lifestyle to me. My mother is a lot like them too. To this day, she frets about spending money. However, as a result of my upbringing, I frequently lack the right tools to do a job.

My grandfather was an incredible handyman who could make almost anything. I did not inherit that skill. When my wife and I have taken on remodeling projects, my wife typically says, "You really try, but you are not your grandfather. So maybe it is better that you leave it to the professionals." Nevertheless, I would muddle through these projects with the wrong tools. Obviously, the job would take twice as long, and the final outcome would be mediocre.

During our last remodeling project, I dreaded the fact that I would have to install trim—floorboards and door frames. Then someone asked if I would like to borrow a miter saw and a nail gun designed for . . . installing trim! My friend showed me how to use the tools and taught me how to apply caulk to cover up errors. With these tools, I suddenly became a pro at installing trim. The process was fast, fun, and satisfying. The angled pieces matched up. The nail gun was precise. I could not believe how much easier the job was with the right tools.

Leaders sometimes expect their teams to do a job but then fail to invest in the tools they need. We can leave them in a daily struggle to achieve a task with a hammer when they really need a screwdriver. The result is that they become dissatisfied with their work and lose respect for us because we won't supply them with the tools needed to solve problems.

We had exactly that problem in our plant, specifically in relation to the quality of our painting processes. About 30 percent of our product needed to be painted again or thrown out as waste. By comparison, our parent company in Japan only needed to repaint 3 percent of the product. We obviously had a huge, costly problem. Worse yet, every other department in our company had to work twice as hard to make up for the poor paint quality. The injection plant had to mold 30 percent more parts than should have been necessary, and the assembly plant was continually delayed because they never had enough parts.

The parent company in Japan constantly sent people to figure out if the problem was our people or the system. In most cases they pointed to our staff. They thought we were not doing the process right.

I wasn't so sure. On seeing the data, we discovered that, in the winter months, the painting quality improved greatly but declined in the summer. When I asked our maintenance manager about this, he calmly said, "The cooling system capacity for the equipment is not sufficient. It can't keep up in the summer months because of the high temperatures and humidity." He added that the new painting system had been installed with the old cooling system—to save money. He had counseled the leaders at that time against this approach, but they did not want to spend the money. The management basically told him to "keep using a hammer to cut down a tree." Then, when management complained about the team's performance, the team kept working, trying to hide frustration and resentment because no one would listen to them.

I took what I had learned to our senior management in Japan. Fortunately, one person was eager to always use the right tools to complete a job. He saw the value of investing in proper equipment. In the end, everyone agreed that our plant was trying to operate without the right tools.

This outcome was very satisfying for our management team. They had long been told that something was wrong with them when, in reality, they did not have the right tools. The company followed through and made a huge investment in solving the problems in the painting system. When the work was completed, it immediately paid for itself. The painting area stabilized and our percentage of flawed product declined to the same percentage as our Japan plant. All the other departments benefitted because they no longer had to compensate for the painting problems.

I am proud to say that our paint department, which at one time was known by our customers to be one of the worst in North America, is now one of the best in the country. Our paint supplier recently told our team exactly that. The team should be commended for doing a great job every day and for their willingness to persevere until they received the right tools.

Make Gradual Improvements (Kaizen)

Leaders who seek to bridge the gap and restore struggling companies must give their team members the right tools. In addition, we have to be willing to listen to them when they tell us they need a new or better tool. Thus, giving people the right tools is strongly connected to the principle of *kaizen.*

Author Bunji Tozawa defines *kaizen* as "changes in methods to make the work easier, conceived and implemented by those who do the work." *Kaizen* encourages people to work together to solve problems. It is the belief that we can always do better, and that just being "good" is not good enough. By establishing an environment where *kaizen,* or continuous improvement, becomes a way of life, small incremental changes can lead to major improvements that can change the direction of an organization.

When we decided to include "making *kaizen* a way of life" in our actions, we had no idea what it would lead to. As the management team embraced the concept and realized it was their responsibility to continuously improve, the team members also applied it. Then everything changed. Many people started to share ideas about how to improve, and they were recognized for those contributions.

I saw that I needed to do more than just pay our staff to motivate them. They needed to be recognized by the company. We began to honor team members publicly each month. As a result, even more people wanted to share ideas. When they identified problems, they didn't complain about them; instead, they provided ideas to fix them. Team members began to fix problems themselves, showing us before-and-after pictures of what they had accomplished. These small, incremental changes improved quality and reduced costs. We could not have achieved our goals without their willingness to share ideas.

Kaizen is central to "opening the bridge" because it leads companies toward gradual and constant improvements that eventually lead to great accomplishments. In my experience, a culture of *kaizen*, combined with having the right tools, sets the team free to be creative contributors.

13

LET THE HORSES RUN

When I moved to Kentucky in the early nineties, I learned about the world of thoroughbred horses. The state is covered with rolling hills and white fences. Big barns house the most beautiful horses in the world.

My wife found a picture of the famous horse Secretariat at a garage sale. She framed it and put it up in one of our bedrooms. Secretariat was an incredible specimen of majesty and power. When Disney released the movie *Secretariat*, I learned what it means to "let the horses run."

A year after that movie was released, I walked through the Murakami doors. It was my second time in Kentucky in almost fifteen years. During those years, I had worked for Japanese companies and I had gained experience in other parts of Asia. While working for several American companies in the region, I was not a foreigner (*gaijin*), but

I was still an outsider, someone who would never be a part of the local system. Those experiences in Asia prepared me for what I was about to walk into.

During my initial days with Murakami, I sensed that my team was holding back. Because of my exposure to Japan, I supposed that this was due to a unique aspect of Japanese culture. The Japanese place high value on working together as a team to the exclusion of individual creativity and independent actions. In fact, a phrase in Japanese says the "the nail that sticks up will be knocked down." There is nothing wrong with this concept within Japanese environments, but when applied to the independent "cowboy," bigger-is-better American culture, problems can emerge.

I noticed those cultural problems right away because I had been involved with Japan for many years. As a *gaijin* (foreigner), I knew I would never be like the Japanese, so I stopped trying to pretend. While working in Japan, I saw other foreigners who were fluent in Japanese trying to *act* as if they were Japanese. From my perspective, it didn't seem natural. I understand the famous phrase, "When in Rome do as the Romans do," but nowhere does it say to *become* a Roman. We each have an identity that is based on our backgrounds and experiences. So, when we try to do something against our true natures, it seems unnatural. My team needed to be set free to be themselves. We needed to

Let the horses run.

My team members seemed to be uncomfortable in their own skins. They had the potential to be thoroughbreds, but they had all become work horses hitched up to pull the plow in the field under the direction of their leaders. This was totally against their nature.

As the company leader in the US, I was the intermediary between the US team and the parent company in Japan. Over the years, I had learned that I could use my status as the *gaijin* in ways that were helpful to everyone on both sides of the world. I sometimes has a "free pass" because I was a foreigner. However, I had to learn how and when to use it.

As a company board member, I figured out that playing the foreigner card produced one of two results. First, I could speak my mind and say what everyone else wanted to say but couldn't for fear of being the knocked-down nail. When I played the card this way, I often saw a lot of heads nodding in agreement. Second, if I said something that was totally off the mark, they would dismiss my thoughts. In these cases, no one paid a big price. After all, I was just a foreigner!

The Japanese managers frequently told me that they didn't understand the American staff. And, despite my efforts to help the Americans understand the Japanese, the Americans struggled to do things the Japanese way. The Americans could never be Japanese, and the Japanese could never be American. This was normal, but the result was frustration and confusion on both sides.

I caught onto this and started to make changes. First we adjusted the roles of the American and Japanese staff. We emphasized that the Americans needed freedom to run the company as their own. But I also wanted the Americans to remember that the Japanese had invested money, technology, and time to establish a great company that would hopefully last for years.

After helping the American's understand their roles, I helped the Japanese understand that their role was to coach local staff without taking control of day-to-day operations. The Americans needed to assume responsibility and they needed the authority to do the job.

Along with these changes, we had to help everyone recognize and understand the cultural differences in the company. Because many of the team members grew up in a farming community, they could use bailing wire and duct tape to fix anything. They were not afraid to get their hands dirty to fix a problem. Obviously, the Japanese team had entirely different backgrounds, with different strengths and abilities. Despite our differences, I believed that we could be unified around our company goals and vision. We needed to accept those differences and "let the horses run."

It helped me to envision a horse in the starting gate, track rails on the left and right, and a finish line. When the horse and jockey head out of the gate, they have one goal: to get to the finish line without breaking any rules. Within the track's boundaries, they have a lot of room to run. Likewise, we could point them to the finish line by setting reachable goals. We could put systems in place based on data, thereby establishing "rails" within which everyone could operate.

This vision became reality. The Japanese learned to loosen their grip and to allow the Americans to lead, to try, and to try again. The Americans agreed to learn from the Japanese. Everyone ran faster. As time went on, the team gained momentum and began to see progress and success. The parent company was pleased with the results, which were the best they had ever seen since the company's inception in 2000. This is what can happen when leaders expect greatness and give people the freedom to run.

I had no idea that seeing those horses in Kentucky, or that watching the movie *Secretariat*, would have such an impact. But I found a team of thoroughbreds, and I learned that leaders have to let the horses run.

EPILOGUE

We expected that 2020 would be a great year for our company. We had just finished a record year for sales and profits. We would celebrate our twentieth anniversary and I would commemorate my ninth year of leading the organization.

Looking at the data, our management team could see that every aspect of our business had improved. Our safety rating had gone from 10.1, which was two times worse than the national average, to less than 0.5. Customer quality had shifted from red to green. Productivity had improved throughout the business: parts-per-manhour had doubled; paint yields had increased from 70 percent to more than 95 percent; downtime went from 3,200 minutes per month to less than six hundred minutes per month; overall scrap went from 4 percent to 0.5 percent of sales.

These improvements allowed us to double our business while reducing our original 2011 headcount. As a result, we could expand and take on new customers. Most importantly, we became profitable. These profits allowed us to pay off our debts and invest back into the company.

We were ready to start the next chapter in our story when Covid-19 started to impact our business. At first, we were not sure what would happen, but we soon realized that we would have to shutter the business for an unknown period of time. I pulled our leadership team together in a room and said that this would be one of the greatest tests we had ever experienced as a company. The only way we would get through it, I added, would be to stay focused on our company vision, goals, and actions.

We agreed to live up to our standard and "treat others like we wanted to be treated." That led us to be completely transparent with our fellow team members. If we received communication from our customers, we would immediately share honest information with them.

There were many uncertain days. Our status seemed to change hourly. But we kept our commitment to the team. I started a regular "Message from the CEO," sharing it internally and on social media so that the community could know what was happening without relying on hearsay.

Eventually, we had to do the inevitable and furlough a majority of our workforce. We debated our decisions as a management team and, on several occasions, they challenged me. At times our discussions were heated and emotions were high. But we continued to lean on our principles. During one of the most heated discussions, I went out to the cafeteria to talk to our team members and to listen to their concerns. They knew that they could eventually get unemployment benefits, but health insurance was going to be a major issue for them. We also heard rumblings in the media about stimulus checks and additional benefits; however, nothing was certain.

After listening to their concerns, I went back to my office and thought about our next steps. I reflected on the comments from the management team and from our team members. I thought about the company's history. I felt strongly that we needed to act, even though I didn't know how everything would pan out.

I gathered the management team again and informed them that we would pay the wages of all full-time, contract, and in-house suppliers for the next two weeks. In addition, we would pay health benefits for the unforeseeable future, including the employee contributions, for all team members regardless of working status. The management team was surprised and grateful. The plan was way beyond what we had discussed.

I believed these actions were a small price to pay for the years of trust and dedication we had received from our team. Their efforts had helped us become profitable and financially stable, which now allowed us to help them during a crisis in ways that other companies could not afford.

Ten weeks later, we started to call people back to work They all came back! They were ready to work and excited to be part of the team. Because our customers had been trying to make up lost production, our team needed to work overtime. They continued to push through that challenge and showed how great they really are.

As I write, some amazing things have occurred. Our customer, Toyota, recognized us with the Superior Launch Award. The local Chamber of Commerce recognized us as its Community Investor of the Year. The local newspaper awarded us with the Best Manufacturing Plant to Work At award. And *Assembly* magazine named us Assembly Plant of the Year. When I saw the list of prior winners, I realized that we were among an elite group of companies.

This book is proof that leaders can "bridge the gap." What has happened in our company is the result of individuals working together as a team. I have been fortunate to be in a position where I could serve as the "keystone" to help them get to the other side, to support them while they built the bridge and implemented the principles described in this book.

There are things that only leaders can do. As long as we are willing to be humble and to recognize that our role is to help others succeed, then hopefully there will be many more opportunities for us to bridge the gaps.

ABOUT THE AUTHOR

Michael A. Rodenberg
CEO Murakami Manufacturing USA, Inc.

Michael serves as the first non-Japanese member of the Murakami Corporation board of directors, as well as CEO of Murakami Manufacturing USA and Mexico. He has a bachelor's degree in Japanese from Brigham Young University and an MBA in global management from the University of Phoenix. Over the past twenty-five years he has worked in the manufacturing industry with assignments in Japan, China, and the US. He enjoys bridging the gap between cultures and organizations, building strong teams, and developing young people.

CPSIA information can be obtained
at www.ICGtesting.com
Printed in the USA
FSHW012213031220
76391FS